INTRODUCTION

Internet users at all levels are looking for an effective cyber-security paradigm. This is the case even as internet usage and infrastructure continues to grow enabling in unprecedented fashion private users to stream media, banks to move money, and governments to conduct their affairs. Unfortunately, crime, exploitation, and invasions of privacy are increasing as well. The cost is billions of dollars and has also resulted in cases of physical destruction. Maybe the best example in this respect, ironically estimated to be of US origin, is the loss of an excessive number of uranium enrichment centrifuges in Iran following the Stuxnet virus.[1] There are a multitude of cyber security issues, but the most important topics address how to define malicious actions in cyberspace, the inadequacy of the international community to address these actions, and how active a role the private sector should play in the overall cyber-security effort.

There is no groundbreaking technology that will solve this problem despite much work by government agencies and corporate entities to do just this. In fact, this effort has compounded the problem in that cyber-security is being examined in its parts when it should be looked at as a whole. This is a distributed problem that needs a distributed answer, a system of solutions that work together as in any well-engineered system. Also, practicality will dictate the speed at which a solution can be implemented. Such a system needs to be comprised of capabilities that exist with today's means for a speedy remedy of money hemorrhaging at the hands of ongoing cyber-crime, and to protect against the next instance of physical destruction where human life may be at risk. The purpose of this study is to propose a holistic solution meeting these requirements by mapping the optimal path through the debates to arrive at a solution set.

EXISTING LITERATURE

As one might expect, no writing addresses the broad picture. Experts offer solutions in the components but necessarily these arguments lack in interaction with each other. Debate can be vigorous in terms of what constitutes an accepted definition of cyber-attack, of the applicability of international law to cyber-warfare, and of the role of the private sector in cyber security. But debate addressing all three of these areas is missing; occasionally two areas will be related, seldom are all three and when it does occur the incidence is coincidental. A usable solution for an effective cyber-security paradigm must include all three, a step this MMS initiates with the understanding that a look at the whole will require a less-than-optimal solution for any one individual area. But this shortcoming is insignificant when the gains of seeing cyber-security as a collective whole are enumerated.

A universally accepted definition for cyber-attack has been heavily sought after to answer exactly what actions in cyberspace characterize an act of war vice actions that are criminal but do not rise to the justification of a state to use force. While cyber warfare is defined by the Congressional Research Service as, "warfare waged in cyberspace," and includes "defending information and computer networks, deterring information attacks, as well as denying an adversary's ability to do the same," and "offensive information operations mounted against an adversary, or even dominating information on the battlefield," it does not help describe the actionable criteria of a cyber attack.[2] Conversely, the Department of Defense avoids the term cyber-warfare altogether and instead offers a definition of computer network warfare. This reads: "The employment of Computer Network Operations (CNO) with the intent of denying adversaries the effective use of their computers, information systems, and networks, while ensuring the effective use of our own computers, information systems, and networks."[3] These definitions describe the nature of military-level operations in cyberspace, but do not offer a measure of warring actions. The leading literature defining a cyber attack is published by the *California Law Review* and addresses the lack of definition with the specificity required for military response by proposing that, "Cyber-attack consists of any action taken to undermine the function of a computer network for political or national security purpose."[4] This important discussion is clearly underdeveloped.

The role of government and the application of international law with respect to cyber-security is another area of much debate. Regarding *jus ad bellum* and *jus in bello,* there have been many comparisons between cyber-warfare and the history of new technologies like aerial warfare or biological weapons to allow moving forward based on a precedence.[5] Despite the complexities of these and other comparisons, current literature simply supports that existing international law either sufficiently addresses cyber-warfare and cyber-attack as it stands, or does not sufficiently address it and needs revision or amendment. There are a few outliers proposing that international law is not applicable to cyber-warfare, or that cyber-warfare is exempt due to inapplicability, but they are not impacting the momentum of current debate.[6] Former Deputy Staff Judge Advocate for U.S. Defense Systems Agency, Davis Brown, published in the Harvard International Law Journal his view that existing international law is inadequate to deal with cyber-warfare and argues for "a comprehensive international body of law regulating information warfare."[7] In direct opposition is the U.S. State Department's Legal Advisor, Harold Hongju Koh, who stated in a September 2012 speech to the U.S. Cyber Command Inter-Agency Legal Conference, that established principles of international law apply to cyberspace, that cyber activities can constitute a use of force, and that jus in bello principles for conduct of war apply to computer network attacks.[8] While a few more voices have surfaced and questioned the definition of cyber-warfare in terms of just war theory, there is no consensus and this literature is very limited as well.

Literature on the role of the private sector in cyber-security is mostly dictated by the Defense Department, but is in keeping with general consensus of civilian outlooks. The third strategic initiative of the Department of Defense Strategy for Operating in Cyberspace includes partnering with the private sector, and is geared toward information sharing and collaborative methods to better defend vulnerabilities. The strategy stresses the importance of working with the private sector for, "increased sharing of information about malicious or unauthorized cyber activity and protective cyber security measures."[9] Bruce Schneier is a leading civilian author writing on cyber-security since the early 90s who promotes information sharing as key to cyber-security. As a cryptographer he believes that every security system can eventually be circumvented, and the increase of users over the last decade from 60 million to over 2 billion people commensurate with the dramatic increase of malicious activities in cyberspace, his emphasis on information sharing is crucial to keeping up with the increase. As U.S. Cyber Command begins a shift towards deterrence by boasting offensive capabilities, offensive operations are seen as a military-only function and not a role for the private sector. Tim Maurer, a research associate for the Center for Strategic and International Studies, goes as far as calling a corporation that conducts intrusive or offensive actions, even in response to an incursion, a cyber vigilante.[10]

With little way forward in the literature, the need for a comprehensive whole is clear. Systems theory offers this way forward, as is explained after a review of the current debates and their complexities. Once it is clear how segmented the conversation has become, a way forward, a systems way forward, can be considered.

GOVERNMENT NORMS AND JUST WAR

First the role of the U.S. government must be considered and justified. The internet is, after all, a private business. There are internet service providers burying fiber, running networks, and servicing hardware to sell subscriptions to users. Users are communicating, and selling goods and services via these networks. The government itself is a paying customer.

A simple view of cyberspace is that it is a line of communication for information and commerce. As a communications medium, the Federal government has been regulating all aspects of domestic and international communication for the United States since the Communications Act of 1934 and the creation of the Federal Communications Commission.[11] More practically, with the amount of money that exchanges hands via the internet every day, and the improved accessibility for merchants to sell their wares via the internet, it has become an essential vehicle of modern commerce.

The previous frontier of commerce also faced a challenge in security. When the world was developing seagoing trade routes, Alfred Mahan pioneered the concept of sea power in the early 1900s which was followed to some degree or another by major seagoing nations. He explained the success of nations as a function of both seagoing commerce and a navy capable of protecting it.[12] Using historical examples, Mahan points out that no single element of the pair alone made for a successful sea power, and that a business advantage is awarded to the more secure sea power. We see an example of this today in websites with trusted systems to handle payment. The more credible a website is, the more likely a customer will be comfortable enough to enter their credit card information and make a purchase even if the price is higher than on a website with unknown credibility. In a more macro view, Mahan also cities French and British naval examples in order to show that a nation's sea power composed of both strong commerce and strong naval protection will allow a nation to survive war and will, at least temporarily, become the only beneficiary of seagoing commerce.[13] If a cyber-war were to break out, a relatively intact cyber commerce system would be vital to a nation's survival. Today, as in the past with sea-born commerce, the proper level of the government's involvement in this world wide private industry needs to be carefully balanced.

An area that is clearly a government responsibility is working with other governments in international efforts to determine the impact of cyberspace on existing international law and just war concept. There is much debate whether current international law is adequate to address issues that come about with the complication of misconduct in cyberspace. In international law *jus ad bellum* addresses when a state is justified in using force, while *just in bello* addresses how a state may conduct themselves in war.[14] Some of the major contention with *jus ad bellum* being able to address cyber-warfare is the requirements that the offended must know where the attack originated from, and that this offense action resulted in destruction of life, property, or other things more physical in nature.[15]

The nature of most cyber-attacks is that they originate from hidden sources often concealing an attacker's motive. Lack of attribution makes meeting this criteria very problematic. Cyber-attacks also do not often result in physical damage. This is where arguments for including intellectual property enter. Intellectual property is most widely understood in the context of multimedia and used by media industries to justify digital rights management and is seen as a business issue, but the concept meets much more sensitive examples. Evidence that classified plans for the F-35 Joint Strike Fighter was stolen from the developing defense contractor by hackers, suspected to be Chinese, shows an action involving intellectual property rights that has a national security effect.[16] Even if the intellectual property argument is accepted, the attribution issue still prevents clear approval for action by the U.S. government against China

on the issue.

Arguments taking place around *jus in bello* do not appear as problematic. The use of

cyber-warfare must meet the same requirements for proportionality and distinction, the

restriction for targeting only enemy forces, as required of the other kinetic tools of war. As long

as these requirements are met, cyber-warfare can be used instead of, or in augmentation of,

kinetic warfare. There are instances like computer attacks that are delivered by virus

indiscriminately infecting, and possibly damaging, other computers it contacts. The most notable

examples of cyber-warfare in augmentation of kinetic warfare is the distributed denial of service

attack against Georgia in 2008 in conjunction with the advance of Russian troops across the

Caucasus; a coordination of effort still only traced to Russian cyber-criminals and not directly to

the Russian government.[17]

The idea of cyberwar treaties, as argued for by noted civilian cryptographer and security

expert Bruce Schneier, was posed to limit the destruction of "cyberweapons" including

prohibited use of un-aimed weapons limiting their effect to only intended targets.[18] Cyber

treaties are not needed in this aspect because limiting effects of any weapon to its intended target

is inherent in *jus in bello* where international law abiding nations must be complicate regardless.

Elements of Bruce's proposed treaty, however, serve as excellent guidelines for manufactures of

"cyberweapons" to present a *jus in bello* compliant weapon such as built in self-destruct features

to limit effect. For *jus in bello* the solution to the debate about cyberwarfare and the use of

cyberweapons is simple. If a weapon, cyber or otherwise, cannot target the enemy it cannot be

used. A solution for the *jus ad bellum* element of the overall problem, however, is much more

complicated and must involve the understanding that without proper attribution, the justification for action by a nation state is not going to happen often and other ways of creating deterrence must be maximized. Bruce's treaty would be a first of its kind and would fill a large hole.

Reaching an understanding in the international community that existing international law does apply to cyber warfare is a task for all governments. Although the applicability of international law to cyber misconduct exists, it clearly cannot justify action against most cyber misconduct. Due to the nature of cyber-attacks, opportunities to justly use force against a nation guilty of conducting an attack will be rare. Unsatisfied, it appears that just war theorists continue to debate application of existing law to more narrow instances of cyber misconduct, or adding to existing international law to allow more capacity to combat the seemingly unbridled cyber misconduct taking place today. Gaining an international consensus will continue to be slow but international cooperation on this issue is more important than ever as the majority of work to combat cyber misconduct needs to take place outside of the realm of war. For now, the international community will have to accept the United States setting the tone and moving forward based off of the minimal framework described above. This is not a bad thing. The minimal framework provides a flexibility that allows for action now while refinement is underway. The important thing is for the international community to continue the dialogue as things progress and as the United States sets precedence while taking any necessary actions to protect the nation. With the United States being a heavily networked country and owning much of the infrastructure, it has the most to lose by way of a cyber conflict. It is reasonable that the United States takes lead. The United States should start with a firm assertion of the definition of key terms. Even if other countries do not adopt these definitions it will at least be clear what actions the United States will consider either a "cyber-attack" or "cyber-espionage."

DEFINING CYBER-ATTACK

Terminology, at first, seems quite straight forward with what appears to be a convention of using existing, well understood words such as, "crime" and, "espionage", and simply adding the prefix, "cyber." Using these cyber words should indicate actions in cyberspace that have the same legal gravity as their conventional root. When looking at these words, however, and when considering what exactly can constitute a cyber-attack, the issue becomes much more complicated. The U.S. National Research Council offers a definition for cyber-attack as, "deliberate actions to alter, disrupt, deceive, degrade, or destroy computer systems or networks or the information and/or programs resident in or transiting these systems or networks."[19] This definition has elements that address a wide range of damage to the physical system and hardware, as well as the software and information.

The U.S. Joints Chiefs of Staff place computer network attack under a broader category called information warfare which is characterized as the effort "to influence, disrupt, corrupt, or usurp adversarial human and automated decision making while protecting one's own."[20] Similarly, the Congressional Research Service defines cyber-warfare as, "warfare waged in cyberspace. It can include defending information and computer networks, deterring information attacks, as well as denying an adversary's ability to do the same. It can include office information operations mounted against an adversary, or even domination information on the battle field."[21] Defining cyber warfare in this way broadens the scope, but makes no mention of actual damage to computers, software, or the loss of information. Nor does it include an aspect of an attack having physical effects such as manipulating a computer controlled device to create real world damage, or being used in concert with a conventional, physical attack to facilitate real world damage.

A competing international definition of war-level cyber activity developed by the Shanghai Cooperation Organization states, "mass psychological brainwashing to destabilize society and state, as well as to force the state to take decisions in the interest of an opposing party."[22] Motivated to protect their governments from social revolution or insurgency, the members of the Shanghai Cooperation (Central Asian nations including China and Russia) consider internet content itself to be a potential threat to cyber security. For the United States and other democratic societies, limiting content implicates freedom of speech issues making this definition troublesome. Can there be a definition that satisfies all international needs?

One solution is to accept different definitions for cyber-warfare, or attack, with an understanding that the definition carries the context of the nation-state that is using it. There is much delay caused by working for international consensus on the matter with the different needs involved. The more a nation depends on networked infrastructure for banking, industrial controls, and commerce, the more it is motivated to concentrate on protecting the hardware and software integrity of the internet and the information carried on it. If a country is more concerned with their own social stability, they are motivated to include terminology and provisions addressing the powerful communication aspects of the internet to protect against its use for, in their view, propaganda.

This problem could be overcome by allowing the various definitions to coexist. However, the need for international consensus is quite valid when you consider that acts of cyber misconduct taking place in one country can originate from within another. If an attack on a computer system residing in the United States is conducted by someone, state or non-state actor, within the physical boarders of another country, it is a problem for both countries to resolve. It is reasonable for the United States to ask for assistance from the country where an attack originated from to bring the attacker to some kind of justice. If the situation were reversed, however, and the country being attacked held the belief that anti-government propaganda was considered an attack, it would be reasonable for them to ask the United States for assistance in quelling the speech of the propagator within U.S. borders who may even be a U.S. citizen. Preventing situations like these is the complication to international consensus costing so much time.

With different requirements and needs within the cyber-security paradigm, there does not appear to be an answer to satisfy all needs, so we must partially satisfy everyone at the cost of not fully satisfying anyone by setting the threshold for what is considered cyber-attack very high. Cyber-attack should be defined as an act of war when it meets requirements of knowing the origination of the attack and destruction and the cause of destruction of life and property. If retaliation at a nation-state level for an act of cyber misconduct cannot be justified by international law, then it is not a cyber-attack. This will serve as a starting point to frame further development over time in just war doctrine.

Terms for all other acts of cyber misconduct, like cyber-espionage, should be considered outside the realm of war and be addressed through international security cooperation. The United States should lead this effort owning most of the infrastructure claiming the largest stake. Boldness is required. It is done so by first making all federal entities abide by the same definitions and terminology. Then, the United States makes a clear statement to the international community that it will enforce against violations of cyber security related to its own people, will assist other countries when cyber misconduct from within the U.S. borders harms them, and ask that other countries do the same. Conducting cyber-warfare and cyber-attack in a just war setting while also combatting all other forms of cyber misconduct in a cyber-security setting is too much for the U.S. Government's capacity, which brings us to the next debate of the civilian role in cyber-security.

CIVILIAN ROLE IN CYBER SECURITY

Private business is a powerful, if not the most powerful, participant in cyberspace. It would stand to reason that the best computer scientists money can buy are working in the private sector where their skills go to work for the highest bidder. When these private companies are exploited or attacked, it is easy for those companies to conduct their own investigation and then counterattack on their own. There is more incentive to take matters into their own hands than reporting it to the government for action because as a business, their vitality relies on a customer expectation of safe and secure transactions of money or storage of customer information. Businesses feel compelled to conduct their own in-house security exploits in cyberspace rather than making their security problem public, thereby risking customer base. This mindset is furthered by a feeling of impotency of the law to do anything about it. In June 2012, Reuters published a report that read, "Frustrated by their inability to stop sophisticated hacking attacks or use the law to punish their assailants, an increasing number of U.S. companies are taking retaliatory action."[23]

Capability combined with incentive gives us examples like Google claiming in January 2010 that they had traced the origin of a cyber attack on China, that also reportedly had exploited several other large names like Adobe and Northdrop Grumman.[24] For a fortune 500 company to not only admit the compromising attack but to announce their own retaliatory hacking effort, Google has taken a bold approach to the issue. However, not all companies that have fell victim or that are in need of protection are internet savvy institutions like Google. These institutions look to the government for security. There is undoubtedly significant cyber capability in the US government with organizations like U.S. Cyber Command which is powered by military and civilian technical experts. But when Cyber Command's duties are expanded to the defense of the entire nation, not just military and government networks, the capability of the private sector to aid in their own defense lies underutilized or untapped.

So how should the private sector be utilized? Opening their systems to government organizations to freely share data is one way of cooperation that is being used today. Usually it is not until after a business sustains an act of cyber espionage that they are willing to do this. When the government does step in and run security for a company or corporation, there are free market implications in that those companies may now have an unfair advantage. For all businesses to be electronically transparent to the government there would have to be legislation in place. The FBI has been seeking legislation to require software manufactures to produce products with a "backdoor" for FBI use.[25] Even if this took place it does not solve the free market issue. Any unfair advantage impacts the global market where foreign companies do not get the same level of protection from a Cyber Command of their own. The solution must protect business without creating an unfair advantage while leveraging the power of government and private industry in cyber-security.

In keeping with the theme that there is no perfect solution but that there is an optimal set of solutions given current options, the U.S. military, specifically Cyber Command, with the coordinated support of other government agencies, should only be responsible for protecting against, and conducting, cyber-attacks and ongoing own-force network defense. This is a seemingly simple idea that appears to follow an understanding of the military's conventional role, but it is important when the private sector's part in this piece of the solution is defined.

Below the line of cyber-attack, companies should be allowed to conduct as much cyber activity in the name of active defense as they can accomplish.

Different than network security where vulnerabilities are continually sought out and patched, in the case of active defense, companies would also be allowed to investigate the source of a compromise so they can remove their stolen data and expose the intruder to the rest of the active defense community. When the counter-intrusion action is reported to the active defense community, an appropriate Federal agency could choose to continue actions based on what was found, the significance of what was stolen, or the identity of the intruder. Whether the intruder is foreign or domestic, a state or non-state actor, the counter-action to hacking into a U.S. business' system is met the same way.

Since attacks and exploitations often come from concealed origins, it is reasonable that the counter action, as long as the action is consistent, does not discriminate. If revealing the origin of an intruder creates complications due to their identity or association, an appropriate Federal agency has an opportunity to take over, but the business is not to blame for defending itself as advertised and expected. By empowering businesses to defend themselves in this way raises the stakes for exploiters and deterrence is created. Larger companies like Google are certainly resourced to accomplish this and smaller companies will most likely outsource their defense to a third party much like businesses already do for their web hosting needs.

To ensure responsibility, businesses that choose to engage in active defense would be required to keep records and be transparent about all defense activities including evidence of attempted or realized compromise and the effect of actions, not necessarily the method itself, taken against intruders. If the government had enough resource to adequately defend the entire nation, this would not be an issue. But removing the helplessness from companies and allowing the military to focus on defense and cyber-attack, this unmanageable problem is distributed across its users. With the civilian sector empowered to defend themselves, and the government providing oversight and dealing with international matters as they are discovered, one can begin to consider how the key security issues in cyber space can be conducted on a day to day basis.

Currently U.S. Cyber Command is responsible for the defense of the nation in cyberspace. They work closely with the Federal Bureau of Investigation (FBI) to help accomplish this regarding domestic matters. Not only does the FBI provide additional manning and expertise, but U.S. Cyber Command belongs to the Department of Defense under U.S. Strategic Command, and can only exercise title 10 authorities under the United States code (USC). Since U.S. Cyber Command is limited to armed forces operations, the FBI brings title 18 authorities, crime and criminal procedures, to bear on the issue. The Central Intelligence Agency (CIA) has its own title 50 authorities and responsibilities they are using to add to the solution as well. The Department of Homeland Security, an integration of 22 departments and federal agencies, is charged with domestic security through title 6 responsibilities.

With foreign state actors, foreign non-state actors, and even domestic actors threatening the nation on a security, economic, and potentially a physical level, the issues exist across all of the titled responsibilities when dealing with cyber misconduct. Short of making a new, all powerful, agency with all the authorities previously mentioned, one organization needs to ensure work and information flow is maximized across all the various entities. Organizationally it makes sense to place one entity in charge of coordination between the rest to ensure consistency and the sharing of information as a problem travels from one titled area of responsibility to the next. With cyber-attack and cyber-warfare definitions elevated to attributable acts of war in a system of solutions, leaving the majority of cyber misconduct to security and criminal institutions already in existence, is a title 10 organization like U.S. Cyber Command the correct pick for an overall in-charge coordinator? The implication of a title 10 organization, armed forces, being the lead organization is that the United States is taking a military approach to dealing with cyber misconduct.

For international norms to work in the cyber age, nations need to move to an inside working outward approach where the violated actively defend themselves. If the motive of the violator is revealed, an appropriate government entity can elevate the issue to take action. A more proper selection for a Federal coordinating entity over all others in terms of cyber security is the Department of Homeland Defense (DHS). DHS, with the responsibility of domestic security through Title 6, is a more reasonable choice to coordinate and have visibility over the whole spectrum of cyber security on goings. Comprised of 22 federal organizations like the Federal Computer Incident Response Center, National Infrastructure Protection Center, CBRN Countermeasures Programs, and even the Secret Service, DHS already has the most diversified security responsibilities and interests. DHS has the wide aperture to coordinate all of the players in cyber security and is more in keeping with our inside-out strategy.

HOLISM APPROACH

There are two concepts used in the sciences that are key to understanding an integrated solution. Holism, and its contemporary form of systems theory, and dynamic programming. Holism was first coined by Jan Smuts in 1962. The concept revolves around the observation that an organism, or system, consisting of many parts behaves in a way that is not apparent when looking at the individual parts it is made of. [26] Holism is defined by Harvard University physician and social scientist Nicholas A. Christakis as, "the abiding recognition that wholes have properties not present in the parts and not reducible to the study of the parts."[27] This is

furthered by "Systems Theory" established in 1969 by Biologist Ludwig von Bertalanffy while

working at the RAND Corporation in an attempt to formalize the understanding of various

systems, their complexities, and interaction of those pieces. [28] When looking at cyber-security in

this manner, it becomes clear that these individual arguments (defining cyber-attack,

applicability of current international law, and the proper role of the private sector) are subset

issues of a larger problem that require a holism approach to understand the entirety of the

system.

A tool in analysis utilizing the holism prospective is dynamic programming. Dynamic

programming deals with understanding multipart problems to arrive at an optimal solution.[29]

Like holism and systems theory, it is used in computer science, mathematics, biology,

economics, and other sciences to reduce recursive work. There is one aspect of dynamic

programming that is particularly pertinent in viewing cyber-security as a system which is, in

dynamic programing, at each decision point in a problem the best, or optimal, decision for that

particular issue may not be the best decision for the whole system. In these cases, a less optimal

decision for the individual case is pursued for the good of the whole problem. To illustrate this

concept *Figure 1* is an example of a very simple dynamic programing example. When assessing

the best path to move from A to E, and assuming a lower number is better, the path between A

and B starts the preferred path. However, since the goal is to get all the way to E the second leg

of the journey must be taken into consideration. Adding the value of the path between B and E,

the total value from A to E, going through B (1 + 9), equals 10. The total value of the path from

A to E, going through C (2 + 5), equals a lesser value of 7 making it the overall better path for

the entire system. Despite the initial path from A to B being the best choice and looking so promising, the best holistic solution for this system requires a path that was not the best solution for the first leg of the total path.

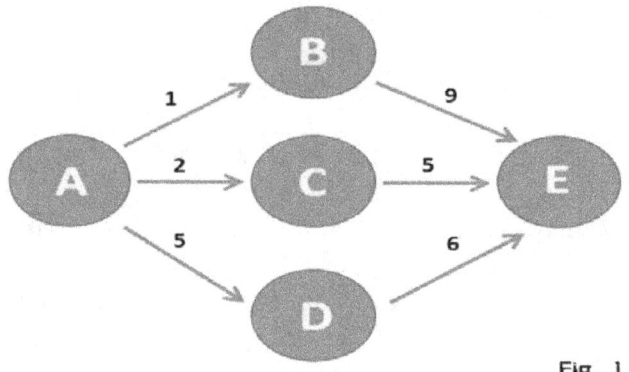

Fig. 1

Taking these concepts and applying them to a cyber-security solution we understand that the answers to the debates of defining cyber-attack, applicability of current international law, and the proper role of the private sector may require a less-than-optimal answer for one or more of the individual debates for the good of the whole system.

Reviewing each debate previously discussed, the need is clear that they need to work together as a system. In the first debate, that of the military's role in an inherently civilian industry comprised of private businesses, we see that there is a historical basis for the military's use by the government to protect commerce. Protection of commerce is in the best interest of the nation as a strong commerce will serve a nation's security.

Interfacing with the other governments in the international community is the next key piece. International debate on the application of just war, *jus ad bellum* and *jus in bello*, to ongoing cyber misconduct, has revealed the major conundrum in aligning cyber misconduct with all other forms in that it is difficult to prove, if at all, the origination of a cyber-attack. What needs to be accepted is that international law applies as is, but that a cyber-attack confirmed to originate from a nation-state is just going to be rarely proven for justification to use force against that nation.

Accepting this, terminology can begin to be brought into consensus. These debates are the least likely to be satisfied with this system of solutions based on all of the different needs of the various nation-states. Vulnerability to social revolution drives more unstable nations to want to control the broadband communication aspect of the internet. For countries where controlling the media is the norm, the internet provides a connection to media outside government control that can be very threatening for them. Due to the borderless nature of the internet, one must rely on help from other nations to police cyber space. For this reason we set the term cyber-attack to mean an unmistakable act of war by current definition. This limits cyber-attack from all that it is currently considered to be, to essentially actions taken against a computer controlled system that result in a kinetic effect. Although a nation could object to what is left out of this definition, no nation could reasonably reject what is in the definition allowing for a commonly understood base for further refinement.

IMPLICATIONS

Given all of the acts of cyber misconduct taking place every minute, and with little justified military action to be taken due to elusive attribution and the failure to meet the act of war criteria, we are left with government agencies and private business to engage in active cyber defense. The internet industry is not bereft of talented computer scientists, and if allowed to counter criminal intrusions, going as far as exploiting the intruder's system, damaging their ability to intrude again, or reveal the identity of the intruder, this step will create a very powerful deterrence. The pressure of getting counter-hacked and possibly revealing a hacker's identity would impose heavy risk to the perpetrator. If the perpetrator is a domestic criminal then they risk being arrested by the FBI or state police. If the perpetrator is a foreign criminal (even a non-state actor) then there is basis to pressure the requisite government to take punitive action. If the perpetrator is a foreign state actor, then justification for the use of military force against that country is at play.

Enabling such private sector "active defense," however, must be done responsibly and is the weakness of this system of solutions. Allowing enough room to accomplish active defense while avoiding collateral damage or businesses taking advantage of this authorization for professional gain will be complicated. Requiring documentation and openness on compromises and active defense actions should sufficiently address most concerns. With oversight from the proper and already existing government organizations, responsible active cyber defense could be maintained and when or if issues need to be elevated to a federal level the mechanism to do so is already in place. The proper government organization consists of one or more organizations exercising their various USC title responsibilities and authorities. A single coordinating entity ensures that the proper organization gets involved at the proper time and facilitates sufficient sharing of information between the others. The Department of Homeland Defense is best suited for those duties as coordination entity.

It is very tempting to shoehorn a military answer for the entire collection of issues that comprise cyber security given the gravity of the issue. In matters where government and military systems are being compromised, or a kinetic effect is an imminent result, military action is appropriate. Those issues exist and are significant, but such actions do not account for the multitude of malicious cyber acts eroding the United States economically or violating privacy. For the latter, working the problem from the inside out by allowing the targets of faceless intruders to actively defend themselves with higher levels of authority (including military) stepping in when justifiably needed, creates a system for deterrence across the board.

Systems theory takes into consideration the interaction between the three issues driving cyber security at present. Since the challenges facing international law in cyber space, the difficulty of defining a "cyber-attack," and the lack of clarity regarding the role of civilian/private sector in cyber-security are being debated separately, experts have not taken their interaction and effect on each other fully into account, leaving the debate compartmentalized and therefore flawed. Depending on how you define a cyber-attack, current international law may or may not be sufficient, and the private sector may or may not have a large role in cyber-security.

For example, the definitions in contention defining a cyber-attack range from very restrictive understandings that only consider a kinetic outcome of a cyber-attack that can be attributed to a specific actor, to very loose definitions that consider the use of the internet to voice political, anti-government propaganda (cyber-activists) as a cyber-attack. If a definition for cyber-attack were selected that was restrictive and only considers attributable kinetic outcomes, then international law is already sufficient when such an event occurs providing a victim nation grounds for action, including kinetic, against the aggressor. The restrictive definition provides a clear operating area for state-level action by government and military that could involve counter-attack, an operating area not suitable for private business and civilians not carrying the proper titled authority by the state / U.S. Code.

Since most cyber misconduct is not attributable, however, the restrictive definition of cyber-attacks keeps grounds for military action narrow and opens a wider range for civilian action against the majority of cyber misconduct seeing how there is no attributable government implication—it is self-defense against a criminal act. Opening up the private sector's operating area to cope with these threats frees up civilian talent for a more significant role in cyber-security. A company actively defending itself by removing or erasing stolen data from an intruder's system is not endangering international law on behalf of its nation because the actions do not satisfy the (now) strict definition for attack. If a less restrictive definition for cyber-attack were chosen, it would change all of these interactions affecting the applicability of current law, possibly requiring revision of law, and would change the scope of civilian involvement effecting the leveraging of civilian talent. This is the level of attention that needs to be paid to the entirety of the cyber-security issue and amount of consideration for the interactions of its pieces. Getting locked into one way of doing things for one issue, although it may be the best solution for that particular issue, limits your options for other pieces and overall effectiveness of the whole.

Systems theory, seeing things as a whole, means that these parts can now look like a comprehensive cyber security effort, in that the civilian element of this new domain does more. The military stays within the lines, as it were, and that means safeguarding the restrictive understanding of cyber defined above. Ultimately, with respect to the civilian role in this, we are asking the nation to defend itself in true fashion—civilians do this. They will do this best by addressing cyber security as a crime until they know it to be a larger matter than simply domestic crime, in which case they then forward the issue the proper government agency. In sum, the efforts of the military to defend the United States speaks to overreach. The civilian side can accomplish much in this respect. Systems tells us that accord between these two entities and doing so according to international law, speaks to a domain that should not be militarized, nor can it.

ENDNOTES

[1] Kim Zetter, "How digital detectives deciphered Stuxnet, the most menacing malware in history," *Wired*, July 2007, accessed 10 January 2013, http://www.wired.com/threatlevel/2011/07/how-digital-detectives-deciphered-stuxnet, 7.

[2] Steven A. Hildreth, *Cyberwarfare*, CRS Report for Congress RL30735. (Washington, DC: Congressional Research Service, June 19, 2001, accessed 9 February 2013), http://www.fas.org/irp/crs/RL30735.pdf, 16.

[3] U.S. Department of Defense, *Information Operations*, Joint Pub. 3-13 (Washington, DC: Joint Chiefs of Staff, February 2006), ix.

[4] Oona A. Hathaway et. al., "The Law of Cyber-Attack," *California Law Review*, California Law Review Inc., 2012, 826.

[5] Davis Brown, "A Proposal for an International Convention to Regulate the Use of Information Systems in Armed Conflict," *Harvard International Law Journal* 47, no. 1 (Winter 2006): 179.

[6] Michael N. Schmitt, "Wired Warfare: Computer Network Attack and the Jus in Bello," *International Review of the Red Cross* 84, no. 846 (30 June 2002): 368.

[7] Brown, "A Proposal for an International Convention to Regulate the Use of Information Systems in Armed Conflict," 181.

[8] Harold Hongju Koh, "International Law in Cyberspace," (presentation, Ft. Meade, MD, September 18, 2012), accessed 12 February 2013, http://www.state.gov/s/l/releases/remarks/197924.htm.

[9] U.S. Department of Defense. *Department of Defense Strategy for Operating in Cyberspace.* Washington, DC: Department of Defense, 2011, http://www.defense.gov/home/features/2011/0411_cyberstrategy/docs/DoD_Strategy_for_Operating_in_Cyberspace_July_2011.pdf, 8.

[10] Tim Maurer, "Breaking Bad: How America's Biggest Corporation Became Cyber Vigilantes," *Foreign Policy Magazine,* 10 September 2012, accessed 24 November 2012, http://www.foreignpolicy.com/articles/2012/09/10/breaking_bad, 1.

[11] "What we do," *Federal Communications* Commission, accessed 24 November 2012, http://www.fcc.gov/what-we-do.

[12] A. T. Mahan, *The Influence of Sea Power Upon History, 1660-1783*, ed. A. E. Warren, (Boston: Little Brown and Company, 1890), The Project Guttenberg eBook, 28.

[13] Mahan, *The Influence of Sea Power Upon History,* 27.

[14] Michael N. Schmitt, "'Attack' as a Term of Art in International Law: The Cyber Operations Context," *Naval War College - International Law Department*, Rhode Island, University of Exeter Law School, 7 September 2012, 284.

[15] James Cook, "Cyberation and Just War Doctrine: A Response to Randall Dipert," *Journal of Military Ethics* 7, no. 9 (2010): 412.

[16] Maurer, "Breaking Bad: How America's Biggest Corporation Became Cyber Vigilantes," 1.

[17] "Cyberwar: The Threat from the Internet," *The Economist*, 1 July 2010, accessed 23 April 2013, http://www.economist.com/node/16481504, 1.

[18] Bruce Schneier, "Cyberwar Treaties," *Schneier on Security* (blog), June 14, 2012, accessed 12 January 2013, http://www.schneier.com/blog/archives/2012/06/cyberwar_treati.html.

[19] William A. Owens, et. al, "Technology, Policy, Law, and Ethics Regarding U.S. Acquisitions and Use of Cyberattack Capabilites," *National Research Council of the National Academies*, Washington, D.C., The National Academy Press, 2009, 1.

[20] Joint Chiefs of Staff, Joint Pub. 3-13, ix.

[21] Hildreth, 16.

[22] Shanghai Cooperation Agreement, Annex I, 209.

[23] Maurer, "Breaking Bad: How America's Biggest Corporation Became Cyber Vigilantes," 1.

[24] Maurer, "Breaking Bad: How America's Biggest Corporation Became Cyber Vigilantes," 1.

[25] Matt Blaze and Suzan Landau, "The FBI Needs Hackers, Not Back Doors," *Wired*, January 2013, accessed 12 January 2013, http://www.wired.com/opinion/2013/01/wiretap-backdoors, 2.

[26] J. C. Smuts, *Holism and Evolution* (New York: The Macmillan Company, 1926), 126.

[27] Nicholas A. Christakis, "What Scientific Concept Would Improve Everybody's Cognitive Toolkit?," *Edge World Question Center*, 2011, accessed 20 January 2013, http://www.edge.org/q2011/q11_6.html, 1.

[28] Ludwig von Bertalanffy, *General System Theory: Foundations, Development, Applications* (New York: George Braziller, Inc, 1969), 7.

[29] Richard Bellman, "The Theory of Dynamic Programming," *The RAND Corporation*, Santa Monica, 1953, 4.

Bibliography

Bellman, Richard. "The Theory of Dynamic Programming." *The RAND Corporation.* Santa Monica: 1953, 1-23.

Bertalanffy, Ludwig von. *General System Theory: Foundations, Development, Applications.* New York: George Braziller, Inc, 1969.

Blaze, Matt, and Suzan Landau. "The FBI Needs Hackers, Not Back Doors," *Wired,* January 2013. Accessed 12 January 2013. http://www.wired.com/opinion/2013/01/wiretap-backdoors.

Brown, Davis. "A Proposal for an International Convention to Regulate the Use of Information Systems in Armed Conflict." *Harvard International Law Journal* 47, no. 1 (Winter 2006): 179-221.

Christakis, Nicholas A. "What Scientific Concept Would Improve Everybody's Cognitive Toolkit?." *Edge World Question Center*, 2011. Accessed 20 January 2013. http://www.edge.org/q2011/q11_6.html.

Cook, James. "Cyberation and Just War Doctrine: A Response to Randall Dipert." *Journal of Military Ethics* 7, no. 9 (2010): 411-423.

"Cyberwar: The Threat from the Internet." *The Economist*, 1 July 2010. Accessed 23 April 2013. http://www.economist.com/node/16481504.

Hathaway, Oona A. "The Law of Cyber-Attack." *California Law Review*, California Law Review Inc., 2012.

Hildreth, Steven A. *Cyberwarfare*. CRS Report for Congress RL30735. Washington, DC: Congressional Research Service, June 19, 2001. Accessed 9 February 2013. http://www.fas.org/irp/crs/RL30735.pdf.

Hongju Koh, Harold. "International Law in Cyberspace." Presentation, Ft. Meade, MD, September 18, 2012. Accessed 12 February 2013. http://www.state.gov/s/l/releases/remarks/197924.htm.

Mahan, A. T. *The Influence of Sea Power Upon History, 1660-1783*, ed. A. E. Warren. Boston: Little Brown and Company, 1890. The Project Guttenberg eBook.

Maurer, Tim. "Breaking Bad: How America's Biggest Corporation Became Cyber Vigilantes." *Foreign Policy Magazine,* 10 September 2012 1-2. Accessed 24 November 2012, http://www.foreignpolicy.com/articles/2012/09/10/breaking_bad.

Owens, William A. "Technology, Policy, Law, and Ethics Regarding U.S. Acquisitions and Use of Cyberattack Capabilites." *National Research Council of the National Academies*. Washington, DC: The National Academy Press, 2009.

Schmitt, Michael N. *'Attack' as a Term of Art in International Law: The Cyber Operations Context*. Rhode Island: University of Exeter Law School, 7 September 2012.

Schmitt, Michael N. "Wired Warfare: Computer Network Attack and the Jus in Bello." *International Review of the Red Cross* 84, no. 846 (30 June 2002): 365-399.

Schneier, Bruce. "Cyberwar Treaties." *Schneier on Security* (blog), June 14, 2012. Accessed 12 January 2013. http://www.schneier.com/blog/archives/2012/06/cyberwar_treati.html.

Shanghai Cooperation Agreement. Annex I. 209.

Smuts, J. C. *Holism and Evolution.* New York: The Macmillan Company, 1926.

U.S. Department of Defense. *Department of Defense Strategy for Operating in Cyberspace.* Washington, DC: Department of Defense, July 2011.

U.S. Department of Defense. *Information Operations.* Joint Pub. 3-13. Washington, DC: Joint Chiefs of Staff, February 2006.

"What we do." *Federal Communications* Commission. Accessed 24 November 2012, http://www.fcc.gov/what-we-do.

Zetter, Kim. "How digital detectives deciphered Stuxnet, the most menacing malware in history." *Wired*, July 2007, accessed 10 January 2013, 1-8. http://www.wired.com/threatlevel/2011/07/how-digital-detectives-deciphered-stuxnet.